Grants and Contracts Handbook

by Dr. Paul C. Holman

Grants and Contracts Handbook (ISBN No. 0-910170-52-5)

Printed in the United States of America (00190500)

For more information and to purchase additional copies contact:
ASBO International
11401 North Shore Drive
Reston, Virginia 22090
703/478-0405

Table of Contents

Preface

One of the roles of administration is to assist the faculty and staff of an institution in the development and administration of grants. Part of this role includes fulfilling an obligation to sponsors who have provided funding for vital activities by providing administrative direction.

By helping improve all aspects of the grants and contracts processes and procedures, the potential to provide up-to-date information and educational opportunities in such matters as human health, jobs, energy, the environment, urban and rural problems, transportation, industry needs, and fundamental areas of knowledge and knowledge transfer for the betterment of the citizens.

This handbook is designed to be a basic reference for grant and contract applicants, executors, project managers, administrators, and staff.

This handbook has been generalized by using the institutional business office as the institutional grants office. Individual institutions may want to restructure the handbook to more closely match their own institutional structure.

The material for this handbook is the result of collecting information and ideas from institutions, agencies, and sponsors throughout the nation for over 20 years, as well as the author's own work. Each of them has added to the body of knowledge about the grants and contracts administration processes, and the author is grateful to them. It is hoped that this handbook will help researchers, institutions, sponsors, and agencies improve the grants and contracts administration processes.

About the Author

Dr. Paul C. Holman is Deputy Chancellor for Finance, The American Educational Complex, Killeen, Texas.

About ASBO

The Association of School Business Officials International, founded in 1910, is dedicated to research, analysis, and dissemination of information regarding improved methods of school business management. Its goal is to educate members in the newest and most accurate management methods, tools, techniques, and procedures. Association activities focus on all areas of school management operations.

ASBO is headquartered in Reston, Virginia, a suburb of Washington, DC.

Preparing an Application

The business office provides the following services:

- Assistance in identifying funding sources.
- Advice about sponsor policies and procedures.
- Help with the administrative detail of completing an application.
- Assistance in securing official approval and signatures.
- Assistance in transmitting applications and the various copies to sponsoring agencies, and to necessary institution locations.

The basic materials you will need to get started include:

- A copy of the sponsor's policy guidelines and application forms.
- This handbook for reference and guidance.

Forms and Formats

Some sponsors provide special forms and instructions for submitting proposals. Others have a suggested format which may be followed.

If a specific format is not provided, the following information should be included:

- Technical description of the project.
- Description of project personnel (vitae).
- Description of facilities available in relation to the proposed project.
- Project time period.
- Budget (use the same format as that shown in Appendix C for each cost activity center).
- Current support, if any, for the proposed project and information concerning submittal of the proposal to other prospective sponsors.
- Cost sharing information, if required by the sponsor.

Tax Exemption

The institution is a nonprofit educational institution exempt from Federal Income Taxes. The institutional Federal Employee Number and the Tax Exemption Number are sometimes required on applications, and may be obtained from the Business Office.

Personnel General Information

This section highlights information relative to general personnel practices applicable to nearly all grant and contract administration requirements.

Employee Classification and Salaries

Sponsor, Federal, and institution policy all provide that people employed on sponsored programs be remunerated in a manner consistent with institution policy to the extent possible and appropriate. Personnel shall be paid the same rate they would receive if they were hired for a comparable position on the regular institutional payroll.

Minimum Wage and Overtime Requirements

The Fair Labor Standards Act of 1938, as amended, requires payment of a premium to non-exempt employees (see Glossary, Appendix A) for all hours worked in excess of 40 in one work week.

For those employees whose normal work week is 37 1/2 hours, straight time pay is given for time worked after 37 1/2 hours and up to 40 hours in a work week.

Federal Law permits hours worked in excess of 40 in one standard work to be taken as compensatory time. The employee has the option of being paid at the rate of time and one-half, or accumulating compensatory time at the rate of time and one-half hours for all hours worked in excess of 40 hours in a standard work week. From time-to-time the institution may place limitations on amounts of compensatory hours that can be accumulated or awarded. Therefore, project directors should ascertain what policies will be in effect at the time the grant or contract will be operable.

To fulfill the obligations of the Act, the employee is required to provide a time record for all hours worked. The employer must retain these records for at least three years.

Under the law, the employer may exempt certain positions from the overtime and record keeping requirements of the FLSA. The requirements for exemption are highly detailed and complex, and include a salary test and job content factors, such as decision-making, supervision, use of independent judgment and discretion, etc. Use of a job title is not in itself sufficient to grant exemption.

Questions about the applicability of the FLSA to specific positions should be referred to the institution Business Office.

Attendance and Leave Accrual

Individuals employed on grants and contracts will follow institutional practice for attendance and leave accrual for vacation, sick leave, personal leave, and jury duty.

While employed on grant and contract projects, individuals may transfer accrued vacation time of up to 10 days with them between projects. Upon termination of employment (as distinct from termination on one account and the simultaneous appointment to another), employees will be paid for accrued vacation time.

Fellowship Recipients Receiving Stipends

Fellowship recipients receiving a stipend from sponsored funds for the furtherance of their education are not employees of the institution, even though payment may be made through the institution. Since they are not employees they do not receive fringe benefits which employees receive, nor is there a benefits charge to sponsored programs for them.

Project Management

This section outlines a number of specific managerial responsibilities which the project director assumes when undertaking direction of a sponsored program. Although specific duties may be performed by other departments, the final responsibility for all aspects of the project are those of the project director.

Payroll Procedures

Payroll checks are processed on a biweekly basis. There is no ''hold-back'' period for regular employees paid on the biweekly payroll. This means that payment is made for work performed through the employee's last work day of each pay period.

Hourly workers, who by contract do not work a full week, are paid for work in the preceding biweekly period. This procedure provides time to certify hours worked prior to payment.

When employees are engaged to work on a sponsored program, funds are encumbered in the amount of the employee's salary for the full period of appointment.

Equipment Control

Items of permanent equipment are often defined by sponsor policy. They are subject to institution and sponsor accountability controls. Revised OMB Circular A-21 raises the amount to $500 for Federal projects and changes the useful life to two years. Some non-federal sponsors have a more restrictive policy. When there is a conflict in definitions, the more restrictive shall be used.

Property accountability control means that the equipment is in the institution inventory, and can be located.

When permanent equipment is purchased, property will be logged by institution property control personnel. Periodic inventories will be required to verify the location of such equipment. The project director must immediately report damaged or missing equipment to the institutional property office.

Title to equipment normally vests in the institution unless the sponsor retains title to the equipment. When required by sponsor rules or contact terms, a final property inventory is prepared by the institution upon the termination of a project and is submitted to the institution Business Office for certification by the project director and/or appropriate officials before it is sent to the sponsor. This is done routinely on many government grants and contracts.

Notice of Legal Action

In every instance where a project director or employee is involved in legal action arising from work on a sponsored program, the institution Business Office must be notified immediately.

Conflict of Interest

Federal and institution guidelines require that grantees establish safeguards to prevent employees from using their positions for purposes that are, or give the appearance of being, motivated by the desire for private gain for themselves or others, such as those with whom they have family, business, or other ties.

Insurance

The institution maintains insurance policies that provide coverage for all sponsored activities. Other coverage must be specifically requested on a project-by-project basis. None of the coverages are designed to substitute for an individual's own insurance policy.

Worker's compensation, general liability, automobile liability, and professional liability are part of the basic insurance coverage extended to projects administered by the institution. There is automatic coverage from the inception of the project. However, there is a need to specifically identify vehicles, boats, aircraft, or facilities acquired in connection with a project so that the institutional insurance carrier can be advised to issue the appropriate policy endorsements. Identification is to be made to the institution Business Office at the time of grant or contract application preparation to determine whether additional premium costs will be required to be added to the grant or contract.

Multiple Project Directors

If a program, grant, or contract is to have more than one project director, the sponsor and the institution will request that one be designated as the responsible party for administrative matters.

The Budget

Where the sponsor provides forms or a suggested format, follow the specified budget categories.

If no budget outline is provided, use the following:

Direct Costs

Personal Services

For institution employees include the following for each individual:

- Job title,
- Rate of pay per annum or academic year (specify),
- Total amount to be paid,
- Fringe benefits for above (consult the Business Office for current rates). This percentage should not be included for consultants and guest lecturers or for students whose employment is beneficial to their educational goal.

When developing budgets use the following example for the format you should use. You will have to obtain exact information from the institution Business Office.

SAMPLE BUDGET FORMAT

1. Part time personnel rate:	
a. Hourly rate	$4.40
b. 20 hours per week	88.00
c. Soc Sec & Retmt @16.5%	14.52
Total	$102.52
2. Full time personnel rate:	
a. Hourly rate	$5.0875
b. Annual rate ($407.26 bi-weekly)	10,582.00
c. Soc Sec & Retmt @16.5%	1,746.00
d. Fringe benefits	3,000.00
Annual Total	$15.328.00

Consultant or Lecturers Fees

A consultant is defined as an individual who is engaged to independently perform a specific job for a stated sum of money, discharging his or her duties with very little supervision and having under his or her own control the manner and detail of accomplishing the end result to be achieved. A consultant may or may not carry out his or her duties at the site of the project. Emphasis here is placed on the completion of a task, regardless of hours and days required.

A lecturer is defined as a recognized expert in a particular discipline engaged to lecture to a group, generally, but not always, to supplement the lectures of the regular instructor. The Federal government almost always requires that the selection process for recruiting consultants be approved by appropriate administrative officials. Whenever such approval is required by a sponsor the proposal writer will be expected to bring the item to the attention of the institution Business Office for appropriate action.

In addition, when the need for consultants is anticipated in the initial development of grant and contract proposals, it is necessary to comply with Federal documentation standards to support the use of consultants. To allow consultant services as direct costs there must be evidence that:

- The services to be provided are essential and cannot be provided by persons receiving salary support under the grant, or cannot otherwise be compensated for their services.
- The charge is appropriate considering the qualifications of the consultant, his or her normal charges, and the nature of the services rendered.

This documentation is required prior to the actual engagement of a consultant and is to be taken into consideration when an individual is preparing the application for a grant or contract.

Since there is a wide range of sponsor policy on this subject, in all cases where there is apparent conflict between the institution and the sponsor policy, the more restrictive shall apply. Questions on consultant or lecturer fees should be directed to the institution Business Office, particularly since Federal sponsor representatives have drawn attention to this subject during fiscal audits.

Equipment

Applications should include requests for equipment categorized in accordance with the following definitions:

- Permanent Equipment -- Those items of equipment (including component parts, etc., but excluding glassware) which have a useful life generally in excess of two years, and whose cost is greater than a dollar level defined by the sponsors policy. The general Federal dollar acquisitioning cost level of $500 per item will usually apply.

- General Purpose Equipment -- Any item of permanent equipment which is generally usable for activities of the project, such as office equipment, reproduction and printing equipment, air conditioners, etc.
- Expendable Equipment -- All items of equipment with a useful life of less than two years not classified in the preceding two categories.

Certain items of equipment should be specifically justified when required by the sponsor, explaining the relationship to the project, such as:

- Permanent research equipment costing $1,000 or more.
- Air conditioners.
- Office equipment: desks, file cabinets, typewriters, calculators, word processors.

Travel

Sponsor regulations generally require that the purpose of proposed travel be explained in detail. When travel expenses of individuals are to be charged against budget funds, the circumstances should be explained. Specific justification for travel differs according to sponsor regulations. Therefore, sponsor policy should be consulted for requirements before budgeting for this category. Travel expenses shall conform to rules promulgated by the institution for institutional employees unless sponsor guidelines are more restrictive. The more restrictive guidelines will apply.

Independent Audit Fees

Certain Federally funded programs require that an audit be performed by an independent certified public accountant. This requirement may exist regardless of whether the project funds are awarded directly to the institution, or whether the institution is subcontracting with an organization which requires an audit.

The costs of individual program audits when required by a sponsor are by definition direct costs and must be included in the application budget. Some examples of agencies which require audits for some or all of their programs are the U.S. Office of Education, and the Department of Housing and Urban Developement. Information regarding the programs which require audits may generally be obtained from sponsor policy booklets. The institution Business Office can provide assistance in determining the proper amount to be included for audits when they are required.

Publications

Costs of publications when permitted by a sponsor are direct costs and must be included in the application budget. Typical publication provisions include:

- Cost of preparation and publication of reports on the research project being supported.
- Reprints of the above.
- Prior sponsor approval is usually required for special charges for early publication of articles, and publication of monographs, books, etc.

Facilities Alterations and Renovation

A detailed justification is required by nearly all sponsors, and usually includes a description of the work, cost estimates, and why the work must be done. The institution Business Office must also be contacted for permission to alter facilities.

Consumable Supplies

Consumable supplies are those used in the normal processes permitted by the conditions specified in the grant or contract. They typically include glassware, chemicals, animals, and other items.

Other Direct Costs

Other items that fall under direct costs, and that are often included in grant and contract budgets are:

- Communications and postage,
- Rental of equipment or space,
- Service contracts,
- Computer time (list type of computer, number of hours, and rate per hour).

Indirect Costs

Each budget should also include an element for indirect costs to cover the expense of providing administration, building space, utilities, janitorial service, libraries, and other comparable and relevant items. Such costs are a recognized charge on almost all Federal research projects, and most sponsors, including private donors, support at least a portion of such costs, although the percentage and method of calculation varies.

The indirect costs appearing in the budget are a negotiated percentage of either the total direct costs, or a portion of the direct costs, such as salaries and wages. The rates used on applications submitted to Federal government agencies are negotiated annually with the cognizant Federal agency and approved by the institution prior to publication and use. For private sponsors, it is necessary to use their published rates.

Any request for waiver of any portion of indirect costs (asking for less than the sponsor will award), must have approval of the institution Business Office prior to submittal of the application. If no indirect costs are permitted, or a limit is set by the sponsor, it is not considered a waiver.

Cost Sharing

Legislation which became effective March 1, 1966, requires that a portion of the cost of research grants from Federal agencies be borne by the grantee institution. Cost sharing is usually not required for projects conducted under contracts. Generally the application should include a statement that the institution will cost share in accordance with sponsor policy. The institution Business Office must also be consulted to determine whether or not the institution will permit the release of such funds.

Matching Funds

Some sponsors impose a requirement that the grantee participate in project costs to a substantial degree by matching fund requirements. The institution Business Office must also be consulted to determine whether or not the institution will permit the release of such funds.

Grant Agreement

A grant agreement is an award document which differs from the usual type of grant award in that an official of the grantee institution must formally accept and acknowledge the award in writing, and agree to the terms and conditions specified by the sponsor.

At the application stage of the funding procedure, it is generally not known whether the resulting award will be made as a grant agreement.

Contract Proposals

A contract, in contrast to a grant, is a binding agreement which requires negotiations and formal acceptance of specific services between the sponsor and the institution. A contract is generally awarded when the sponsoring agency conceives the project and seeks a specific service or solution. Whereas a grant, on the other hand, is generally the instrument awarded by a sponsoring agency pursuant to submittal and approval of a proposal conceived by a faculty member.

Many sponsors utilize both grant and contract formats and at the application phase of seeking funds it is not always known whether a proposal will result in a contract or grant. Funding notices which call for a specific objective will normally result in the issuance of a contract.

In preparing the budget portion of a contract proposal, it should be noted that the mandatory cost sharing associated with Federal grants is usually not a requirement when applying for Federal support. However, it may be necessary and/or desirable to show the institutional contribution to the project.

Contracts are generally of two types. The fixed price contract stipulates that the award for the work to be preformed will be made in a total amount, not generally subject to change. The cost reimbursable contract is one in which the sponsor will reimburse the institution for expenditures made on the project up to a specific limit, often referred to as a ''ceiling'' amount.

CHECKLIST FOR PROPOSALS

There are seven principal areas that should be checklisted whenever a proposal is prepared:

- Are the necessary institutional approvals provided?
- If a subcontract is involved, is the period of the subcontract appropriate, and does it include all costs of the subcontractor?
- If the proposal results from a response to an RFP (requests for proposal/price), have all of the RFP conditions been completely met?
- Are all attachments referred to in the proposal present?
- Do the sponsor's regulations conform to the institutional policies regarding patents and copyrights?
- With regard to human subjects, have all institutional policies been observed?
- Does the overall budget compute correctly, including the appropriate fringe benefit and indirect cost amounts?

Deadlines

When considering sponsor deadline dates, note requirements for either receipt or postmark dates, and allow sufficient time for application processing and mailing. Also, allow adequate additional time for required institutional reviews.

Time Extensions

Extensions of time with no increase in funding are sometimes required to complete a program satisfactorily. Most sponsors ask that requests for such extensions be submitted at least three months prior to termination of the budget period.

Time extension requests must receive proper institutional administrative endorsement before being forwarded to the sponsor.

Absence of Project Director

If the project director expects to be away from the institution for a significant period of time, an explanation of how the supervision and administration of the project will be sustained is requested by most sponsors, and is required by the institution.

Proposal Evaluation by Sponsor

A sampling of the criteria used by the various sponsoring agencies in evaluating research proposals is provided here to aid in the preparation of the technical aspects of proposal writing.

There are many sources available for technical and scientific advice on a prospective proposal. Colleagues, for instance, can offer their opinions and suggestions on subject matter and text. The institution Business Office can provide guidance in connection with the proper forms, formats, and procedures to follow, and there are many books and articles offering advice on this subject. Most sponsors are willing, and often prefer, to discuss new proposals and ideas with prospective project directors prior to the preparation and submission of a formal application.

Principal Reasons for Grant Disapproval

Class I Problems -- Project

- The problem is of insufficient importance, or is unlikely to produce any new or useful information. The proposed research is based on a hypothesis that rests on insufficient evidence, is doubtful, or is unsound.
- The problem is more complex than the investigator appears to realize.
- The problem has only local significance, or is one of production or control, or otherwise fails to fall sufficiently or clearly within the general field of the sponsor.
- The problem is scientifically premature and warrants at most only a pilot study.
- The research as proposed is overly involved, with too many elements under simultaneous investigation.
- The description of the nature of the research and of its significance leaves the proposal nebulous and diffuse, and without clear research aim.

Class II Problems -- Approach

- The proposed tests, or methods, or procedures are unsuited to the stated objectives.
- The description of the approach is too nebulous, diffuse, and lacking in clarity to permit adequate evaluation.
- The overall design of the study has not been carefully thought out.
- The statistical aspects of the approach have not been given sufficient consideration.
- The approach lacks imagination.
- Controls are either inadequately conceived or inadequately described.
- The materials the investigator proposes to use are unsuited to the objectives of the study or are difficult to obtain.
- The number of observations is unsuitable.
- The equipment contemplated is outmoded or otherwise unsuitable.

Class III Problems -- Investigator

- The investigator does not have adequate experience or training, or both, for the proposed activity.
- The investigator appears to be unfamiliar with recent pertinent literature or methods, or both. The investigator's previously published work in the field does not inspire confidence.
- The investigator proposes to rely too heavily on insufficiently experienced associates.
- The investigator is spreading himself or herself too thin. He or she will be more productive if he or she concentrates on fewer projects.
- The investigator needs more liaison with colleagues in this field, or in collateral fields.

Class IV Problems -- Other

- The requirements for equipment or personal, or both, are unrealistic.
- It appears that other responsibilities would prevent devotion of sufficient time and attention to this research.
- The institutional setting is unfavorable.
- Research grants to the investigator, now in force, are inadequate in scope and amount to cover the proposed research.

PROJECT PROPOSAL TIPS

- Start with a researchable problem; one that can be done. Write clearly and in sufficient detail to explain what the project seeks to do. Keep the language simple and to the point.
- Never assume under the evaluation process that the reviewers will accept intent. When clarity is lacking, the consensus will generally be that the initiator of the proposal is not informed or is naive.
- Start out with a clear research aim.

Budget Administration

After a grant or contract has been awarded, the project director is responsible for the conduct of the project. The following items will assist the project director in the daily conduct of the project.

Non-Personnel Expenditures

In addition to the employment of project personnel, it is the responsibility of the project director, with the assistance of appropriate offices, to expend award funds necessary for supplies, equipment, consultants, subcontracts, travel, and other items needed to carry out the project activities.

Ordering Supplies and Equipment

All orders should be handled in accordance with regular institutional procedures. All purchasing of supplies and equipment is initiated by completing a purchase requisition (purchase order) form. When this form has been signed by the project director, it is sent to the institution Business Office for processing. The institution Business Office will verify that the award terms, sponsor guidelines, available funds, and Federal purchasing regulations permit the purchase requested.

In some cases, it may be necessary to seek prior approval from the sponsor for the purchase. In others, prior institutional approval must be observed.

Assuming that all is in order, a purchase order is produced. Orders for supplies and equipment will be placed with the vendor by those responsible for purchasing at the institution. When a vendor is a sole source of supply, the project director should make this known to the Purchasing Office, and the justification for the sole source should be documented in the procurement file for future audit.

In some cases, the purchase order alone is not sufficient for ordering all types of goods or services. In the case of purchase orders involving complex or specially fabricated items of equipment, they would not fully protect the interests of the institution, the sponsor, and the project's schedule and objectives. To ensure that the exact requirements are fulfilled, the institution should enter into a written contract with the vendor of the item, setting forth the special requirements and other appropriate conditions that protect the interests of the institution. These requirements may include performance, standards, delivery dates, payment schedules, guarantees of workmanship, etc. Both parties to the contract must agree to its terms before the work begins and, therefore, the institution has no obligation to pay any costs until all terms and conditions are agreeable to both parties involved. There are a number of other instances when a purchase order will not suffice as the document to be used in the procurement process. When contracts or some other form of written agreement are required as part of the purchasing process they may be included as an addendum to the purchase order.

Project directors are urged to avoid making any commitments directly to vendors, because such action may inadvertently violate a sponsor or institution requirement regarding purchasing procedures.

The project director receives two copies of the purchase order. One of these is a file copy, and the other is a receiving copy. The latter is to be signed and dated, and returned to the institution Business Office when the ordered material has actually arrived, and the project director has determined that there has been no breakage or shortages in the order. If the project director finds the order is not complete, or that there has been breakage, the institution Business Office should be notified of the problem.

It is most important that once an order has been accepted, that the receiving copy be processed immediately so that the vendor can be paid, discount can be taken, and the integrity of the account maintained. When the receiving copy of the purchase order and the vendor's invoice have been received by the institution Business Office the Purchasing Office will be contacted for file verification and closure, and payment authorization will be forwarded to the Business Office.

To expedite delivery of materials ordered, project directors are encouraged to:

- Ascertain that the materials are allowable purchases under the terms of the grant or contract.
- Ensure that there are sufficient funds within the appropriate budget category of the award to cover the order. If not, contact the Business Office for advice, or for possible rebudgeting action.
- Consult sponsor regulations if it is necessary to deviate from the equipment requirements included in the application and/or approved in the award, so that any necessary approvals are obtained.
- Order as far in advance as funds and planning will permit. To obtain sufficient lead time for complex purchases, contact the institution Business Office even before the effective date of the award, especially when bidding is required.
- Assure that the purchase requisition contains accurate data, particularly such items as account number, a complete description of the material desired, and the delivery point.

Closing the Project

This section summarizes reports which must generally be submitted to project sponsors at the end of an award period, with the disposition of unexpended funds, and with audit processes.

Final Fiscal Report

The final fiscal report summarizes the financial activities on the award from its inception. The report is the end-product of all expenditure information from the time an account is established until it terminates.

Depending upon the type of award or the sponsor, the final fiscal report is normally due within 90 days.

It is the project director's responsibility to ensure that all materials and/or services have been received or rendered, and that all expenses are paid from the awarded funds as soon as possible after project termination. Late filing of reports can result in sponsor action to withhold final payments or renewal awards.

A frequent cause for delay in submitting the final report to the sponsor is the existence of unpaid purchase orders. It is advisable to keep a close watch on outstanding purchase orders to ensure that needed materials are delivered and paid for promptly.

Technical Reports

The requirements for technical reports vary from sponsor to sponsor. Report requirements are set forth in grant terms and conditions or, in the case of contracts, are incorporated in the contract language.

The institution has a responsibility for ensuring that requests for technical reports are fulfilled, but the preparation of the technical report is the project director's responsibility.

Unless technical reports are filed within the time allotted by the project sponsor, there may be delays in receiving payment for program expenses. In addition, if technical reports are not filed in a timely fashion, there may be an adverse effect on applications for new funding.

Disposition of Grant Balances

The disposition of any balance remaining in the grant is determined by sponsor regulations, and will be processed accordingly at the same time the final fiscal report is completed.

The unobligated balance in most grants or contracts funded by Federal sponsors is returned to that sponsor. Also returned to the sponsor are balances in grants funded by most other organizations.

At times it may be possible to carry unexpended balances forward to a new grant period. However, this is never done in a way that would increase the next period funds available for expenditure unless specific prior arrangements are made with the sponsor.

Balances in those accounts which have been awarded on a ''fixed price'' basis are transferred to specific accounts set up for that purpose. A similar situation occurs with grants which have small balances which the sponsor does not require be returned.

There is always the possibility of exceptions to these general guidelines based upon specific conditions set forth by a particular sponsor in the award notification or subsequent correspondence. For this reason, as with other aspects of project management, any questions which arise should be referred to the institution Business Office.

Audit

The project director and Business Office are responsible for maintaining auditable records and for interacting with auditors with respect to the propriety of charges, and the application of sponsor and institution policies.

Special Research Considerations

There are several special situations that have arisen in recent years that require special consideration.

Use of Human Subjects

State and Federal laws require that all applications, including requests for renewals and continued support, that involve the use of human subjects be reviewed and certified by the applicant's local institution human subject review committee, regardless of whether the sponsor requires this information.

Human subject means any individual who may be exposed to the possibility of injury, including physical, psychological, or social injury, as a consequence of participation as a subject in any research, development, or related activity. Many other non-Federal agencies require that research be carried out in accordance with these guidelines.

The institution requires adherence to the preceding paragraphs, and will seat a Human Subject Review Committee/Board whenever necessary. Institutional review will be required prior to submission of the application.

All pertinent proposals must include, among other requirements, a ''Memorandum of Understanding and Agreement'' certifying that an Institutional Biosafety Committee has reviewed and approved the facilities, procedures, practices, training, and expertise of the personnel involved in the proposed research. The institution will seat such a committee whenever necessary.

Research Involving Recombinant DNA Molecules

State and Federal agencies have adopted guidelines with respect to the administration and conduct of research involving recombinant DNA molecules. The institution requires adherence to these guidelines.

All pertinent proposals must include, among other requirements, a ''Memorandum of Understanding and Agreement'' certifying that an Institutional Biosafety Committee has reviewed and approved the facilities, procedures, practices, training, and expertise of the personnel involved in the proposed research. The institution will seat such a committee whenever necessary.

Other Areas of Concern

Various State and Federal regulations exist concerning animal use, radiological safety, biohazardous materials, and controlled substances. There may be a requirement for additional reviews to ensure compliance with these regulations. The institution will expect the grant originator to bring these regulations to the attention of the institution Business Office which will prepare proper procedures.

Appendix A

Glossary

Account -- A systematic record of the financial transactions pertaining to an individual award.

Account Expenditure Summary -- A monthly financial status report on a project showing actual current month expenditures by category of expense, cumulative expenditures to date, and encumbrances and unencumbered balance of direct and indirect costs. In addition, the total budget of each category of expense is shown as well as payroll detail, open purchase orders, cash received, accounts receivable balance, and other information of a financial nature of interest to the project director and the institution.

Advance Expenditure Authorization -- A document issued by the institution authorizing expenditures to be made against an account in anticipation of the receipt of a formal award notice.

Affirmative Action Terms -- The following terms are those usually used in affirmative action correspondence:

Affirmative Action -- Any activity undertaken by an employer which ensures equal employment opportunity for minorities, females, the elderly, and the disabled, including, where appropriate, establishment of goals to correct underutilization, correction of problem areas, etc.

Disabled Veteran -- A person entitled to compensation under laws administered by the Veterans Administration for disability rated at 30 percent or more, or a person whose discharge or release from active duty was for a disability incurred or aggravated in the line of duty.

Ethnic Identity -- Post employment information as to race of employees gathered by visual survey. This information, which the Federal government requires Federal contractors to provide to the government annually, is based on EEO categories.

Handicapped Person -- An individual who (1) has a physical or mental impairment which substantially limits some or more of such person's major life activities, or (2) has a record of such impairment, or (3) is regarded as having such an impairment. In the employment environment, a handicapped person is ''substantially limited'' if he or she is likely to experience difficulty in securing, retaining, or advancing in employment because of handicap.

Veteran of the Vietnam Era -- A person who served on active duty for a period of more the 180 days, any part of which occurred between August 5, 1964 and May 7, 1975, and was discharged or released therefrom with other than a dishonorable discharge; or who was discharged or released from active duty for a service-connected disability if any part of such active duty was performed between August 5, 1964 and May 7, 1975, and who was so released or discharged within 48 months preceding an alleged violation of the Vietnam Era Veteran's Readjustment Assistance Act of 1974, the affirmative action clause, or the regulations issued pursuant to the Act.

Application Disapproval Date -- the date on which a proposal is rendered inactive for one of the following reasons; withdrawal by the sponsor or project director, disapproval for scientific reasons by the sponsor, insufficient funds by the sponsor, or stale dating (i.e., a routine closing after review, which takes place 60 to 90 days after a project end date).

Application Proposal -- A formal written request to a funding agency to support a project. It normally describes plans for, and objectives of, the project, as well as the costs involved, and the methodology necessary.

Application Continuation -- A non-competitive proposal submitted for continuation of a specific project previously administered, and where the sponsor has recommended future support for the budget period being requested.

Application New -- A proposal submitted for support of new projects.

Application Renewal -- A competitive proposal submitted for continuation of a specific project previously administered, and where the sponsor had not recommended future support for the budget period being requested.

Application Supplemental -- A proposal submitted for additional funds for the current budget period of the project.

Award -- A designated amount of funds in the form of a grant or contract committed by a sponsor to support a project.

Budget Category -- A classification of a specific element of cost within an account.

Cognizant Audit Agency -- The Federal audit agency designated to perform audits on all federally supported programs, including direct and indirect costs proposals.

Commitment Encumbrance -- Obligations incurred in the form of orders, contracts, and similar items that will become payable when goods are delivered or services rendered. The term is synonymous with encumbrance.

Committed Funds -- The total funding available for expenditures regardless of the source of the funds or the nature of the award instrument. They include booked awards, carry-forward funds, indirect costs, advance expenditure authorizations, and funds provided from other sources.

Computer Software Licensing --This is a new form of license that is assuming increasing importance. The development of a computer program can be a long and expensive exercise, or demand special skills that are not generally available. It is becoming quite common for licenses to be given that grant to another the rights to use or reproduce computer software that has been patented or copyrighted. Since it is difficult for the licenser to know how many times the program has been used and what royalties are due, the license is usually granted in return for an outright payment.

Consultant -- A consultant is an individual who is engaged to perform, independently, a specific job for a stated sum of money, performing his or her duties with very little supervision, and having under his or her own control the manner and detail of accomplishing the end result to be achieved.

Contract -- A binding agreement which requires negotiations and formal acceptance of specific terms for specific work performance and/or services between the sponsor and the institution.

Copyright -- The copyright system began to evolve at the end of the eighteenth century to prevent the extensive pirating of books, songs, and artistic works that was occurring at the time. Until recently, copyright was defined as an exclusive legal right to reproduce, publish, and sell original written and artistic works for a 28 year period in the United States, and renewable for an additional 28 year period. However, a new law, which became effective January 1, 1978, increased the second period from 28 to 47 years for works already under statutory protection. For works created after the new law became effective, the term lasts for the author's life plus an additional 50 years. For works made for hire, or anonymous works, the term is 75 years from publication, or 100 years from creation, whichever is shorter.

After January 1, 1978, all works are copyrighted under the Federal statute upon creation in a tangible form. Although registration with the U.S. Copyright Office and use of the accepted notice are not conditions for securing the initial rights, ''registration'' and ''notice'' are still important. A generally suitable notice is to mark the work with a (c), the author's name, and the date. If the notice formality is not observed upon publication, protection may be affected and the automatic copyright lost.

Registration is only necessary when there may be litigation and is with the U.S. Copyright Office, which is part of the Library of Congress. The procedure is fairly simple, but a good clean copy of unpublished works must be available, and two copies of published works. Like the patent system, the most important aspect of copyright is that it excludes others from enjoying the rights accorded to the author or artist.

In recent years, the development of computing has caused some overlapping between the copyright and patent systems. Although inventions related to computers are usually patented, the programs or "software" can be copyrighted. It is still, however, often up to the courts to make the final decisions in some areas such as electronic games, i.e., "firmware."

Copyrighting Software -- The procedure for copyrighting software is not fundamentally different from that used for copyrighting more conventional materials. A normal notice on the piece of work is again (c), the author's name, and the date. The processes or methods embodied in the program are not copyrightable, but the mode of expression adopted by the programmer is the copyrightable item. Since the law is sometimes hazy and difficult to enforce, many owners of software prefer to use confidentiality provisions rather than copyright to protect their rights.

Many computer programs become obsolete so fast that it is often not worth going through the deposit procedure. However, as with any copyrighted material, there may be a future requirement for deposit so that two good clean copies should be set aside and retained in case they are ever needed.

Cooperative Agreement -- An agreement between two or more parties to cooperate in a set of defined activities or project, involving mutual and shared responsibilities in the planning, objectives, and conduct of the project.

Cost Sharing -- That portion of project costs which, under terms of the award, are required to be contributed by the grantee in the form of direct or indirect costs which may be in cash, in kind, or both, derived by the institution and/or third party institutions, organizations, or individuals.

Direct Costs -- Those costs that are specifically identified with a project. They include salaries and wages, fringe benefits, equipment, publication expenses, and others.

Employee -- An individual who performs services for the institution for which he or she receives wages or salary.

Encumbrance Commitment -- See **Commitments**.

Endorsing Designee -- A senior official designated by the president of the institution to endorse an application, ensuring that the project is acceptable from a campus viewpoint, and assuring that the application conforms with current budget and other fiscal policies.

Fellow -- An individual who is paid stipends from sponsored funds, and who may or may not have an employee/employer relationship with the institution. These funds are treated as a "gift" in recognition of the scholarly potential of the individual for the purpose of enhancing his/her knowledge and training in a field or specialty.

Fellowship -- Financial assistance awarded primarily on the basis of academic achievement and vocational and/or professional objectives.

Final Fiscal Report -- A final certified accounting of the expenditure of funds of an award, usually produced in accordance with regulations or requirements of the sponsor.

Fiscal Designee -- The fiscal designee is responsible for certifying all transactions involving payments from sponsored funds, thereby assuring campus control over the use of project funds.

Grant -- An award normally made by a sponsor pursuant to submittal and approval of a formal application setting forth plans and budgets for the accomplishment of a stated objective.

Grant Agreement -- An award made by a sponsor which requires the grantee to provide written acceptance of special terms and conditions.

Grantee Institution -- An institution identified as having the legal responsibility for fiscal administration of sponsored funds, including the receipt and expenditure thereof, in accordance with established policy and the terms and conditions of the award, and the rendering of such fiscal and other reports as may be required by the sponsoring agency.

Guidelines -- Outlines by a sponsor setting forth its special and procedural regulations regarding policies and procedures.

Indirect Costs -- Those costs which by nature are not readily identifiable with particular projects, but are nonetheless absolutely necessary for their performance. They include providing administrative service, operating and maintaining buildings and equipment, expenses for utilities, janitorial services, libraries, etc.

Invention -- An invention is a new device, process, composition of matter, or even, in some cases, a new use or application of an existing device or process. An ''invention'' has no legal status as a patent does. Improvements or new uses may also be inventions, and in some cases may convert an existing, but non-commercially viable, invention into a profitable and sought after product.

In cases of doubt as to whether an invention is patentable or otherwise protectable, it is usually better to secure legal opinion rather than publishing the information precipitously and risking losing valuable rights.

Lecturer -- A recognized expert in a particular discipline, engaged to lecture to a group.

License -- A license is usually the grant by a patent or copyright holder to another party of any or all of the rights under the patent or copyright. This is normally done for a financial consideration which can take a variety or forms ranging from a onetime payment to many types of royalties or a cross-license to an equally valuable piece of intellectual property. It is important to note that ''know-how,'' trade secrets and other proprietary rights can also be the subjects of valuable licenses. There has been an increasing trend in recent years for governments to force owners of intellectual property to grant licenses when it is deemed to be in the public interest. This has been particularly true of pharmaceutical products in developing countries.

Mainframe -- Generally a large centrally located computer.

Matching Funds -- That portion of project costs in an amount stipulated by the sponsor which, as a condition of an award, the grantee agrees to provide in cash, in kind, or both, derived from the institution and/or third party institutions, organizations, or individuals.

Non-Exempt Employee -- Generally refers to classified or technical employee classifications.

Patents -- The present patent system was developed over the last 200 years in the United States and elsewhere to protect the rights of inventors to their discoveries. In return for disclosing full details of the invention in the patent application, the U.S. Government may grant the inventor a patent which permits him/her to prevent anyone else to make, use, or sell the invention in the United States without his/her permission. A United States patent is valid for 17 years from the date of issue, and the three main criteria for patentability are non-obviousness, novelty, and utility. Most other countries have similar patent systems, although the duration of the patent may differ.

There are international agreements governing patent law and the date of filing in any of the leading industrial countries is accepted as the filing date in the others. The United States patent law does, however, differ from most countries in two important respects. First, in the case of simultaneous invention, the courts may award the patent to the inventor who first reduced the idea to practice rather than the first person to file the application. It is essential, therefore, that potential inventors maintain well-documented records that have preferably been signed by independent witnesses. Second, in the United States, even if the invention has been disclosed to the public, it is still possible to apply for a patent for one year following the date of disclosure. Rights in almost all foreign countries, however, are irrevocably forfeited once a public disclosure is made anywhere in the world (and now, probably, outside the world). Potential inventors should, therefore, carefully consider the possibility of patenting well in advance of making any oral or written disclosure of their research results or discoveries.

Project -- An organized undertaking in an area of the project director's specific interests and competencies.

Project Director -- the individual who has been designated to direct the program a sponsor has agreed to support. The individual is considered responsible for the conduct of the project under the terms of the award and the policies of the institution. Sometimes referred to as the principal investigator.

Proposal Application -- A formal written request to a funding agency to support a project. It normally describes plans for and objectives of the project as well as the costs involved.

Real Time -- An environment in which the receiving of data, processing of data, and taking action or returning results, is done sufficiently fast to produce an effect at that time.

Sponsor -- Any public or private entity or individual offering funds to support research, training, etc., through the institution which utilizes members and facilities of the institution to accomplish the stated goals.

Stipend -- A payment made to an individual to defray living expenses while in training or participating in project activity. The primary purpose of the payment is that of furthering the education or training of the recipient. The payment represents a gift of money for the furtherance of education.

Trademark -- A trademark is a name that identifies a particular brand of product. Trademarks must be used as adjectives and are normally identified by capitalizing the first letter of the mark and putting a small ''TM'' after the word, or preferably, if the trademark is registered, by putting an ''R'' after it. Registration is done by a recognized legal procedure, but one requirement is that the trademark must have been used in genuine interstate commerce. A well-known trademark is a very valuable piece of property, and is sometimes licensed.

Appendix B

Internal Approval Form

To Be Submitted with a Proposal

Principal Project Director: ______________________________
Department: ______________________________
Phone: ______________________________

Project Title: ______________________________

Application: _______ New _______ Continuation
_______ Renewal _______ Supplemental

Period: Start Date: ___/___/___ End Date: ___/___/___

Activity Summary: ______________________________
____
____

Sponsor: ______________________________

Budget Summary:

	Sponsor	Institution	Total
Direct Costs:	________	________	________
Indirect Costs:	________	________	________
Total Costs:	________	________	________

Approvals:
Project Director: ______________________________ Date: ___/___/___
Supervisor: ______________________________ Date: ___/___/___
Director: ______________________________ Date: ___/___/___
Assistant Superintendent: ______________________________ Date: ___/___/___
Grants & Contracts Officer: ______________________________ Date: ___/___/___
Superintendent: ______________________________ Date: ___/___/___
President of the Board: ______________________________ Date: ___/___/___

Copies: Original: Project Director
Office of Record: Institution Business Office

Appendix C

Budget Categories

When constructing budgets one should keep the following most often used budget categories in mind. It is helpful if you note these account categories as well as the amounts on your budgets. An example of a typical institution follows:

2100	**Salaries** (administrator, technician, secretary, student)
2181	**Social Security & Retirement** (16.5% of all salaries except students)
2182	**Fringe Benefits** ($3,000 for all full time employees)
2212	**Contracted Services** (if you plan to use a regular employee on a contract basis, plan to pay the 16.5% out of the contract)
2261	**Tuition Grants** (to cover student tuition and fees)
2311	**Classroom Supplies** (note: whenever you purchase supplies with grant funds you must have a grant number on the P.O)
2314	**AV Supplies**
2353	**Office Supplies**
2355	**Printing**
2359	**Photography**
2234	**Instructional Repair**
2251	**Office Repair**
2516	**Mileage** (keep records on standard forms)
2541	**Telephone Costs** (keep long distance call record)
2543	**Postage**
2518	**Travel & Conference** (keep meticulous records)
2533	**Publication**
2534	**Advertising**
2411	**Building Rental**
2412	**Equipment Rental** (in some instances the institution has purchased equipment, and then leased to the grant. The rental figure must be at least as large as the cost of the equipment.)
2471	**Building Insurance**
2472	**Liability Insurance**
2820	**Office Equipment Purchase**
2821	**Classroom Equipment Purchase**
2824	**Audio Visual Equipment Purchase**
2828	**Textbook Purchase**
2840	**Computer Purchase**

Appendix D

Protection of Human Subjects

Assurance Certification Declaration

1. Activity Title: ____________________
2. Principal Investigator: ____________________

3. Declaration that human subjects would or would not be involved:

_____ A. No individuals who might be considered human subjects, including those from whom organs, tissues, fluids, or other materials would be derived, or who could be identified by personal data, would be involved in the proposed activity.

_____ B. Human subject would be involved in the proposed activity as:
_____ 1. Minors
_____ 2. Fetuses
_____ 3. Abortuses
_____ 4. Pregnant Women
_____ 5. Prisoners
_____ 6. Mentally Retarded
_____ 7. Mentally Disabled
_____ 8. Other (specify)

4. The Institutional Human Subjects Research Review Committee hasdetermined:
_____ A. Human subjects will not be at risk.
_____ B. Human subjects will be at risk.

5. The Institutional Human Subjects Research Review Committee recommends:
_____ A. The proposed research should be permitted.
_____ B. The proposed research should not be permitted.

Comments/restrictions/recommendations:
____
____

6. Signatures:
A. ____________________ Date: ___/___/___
Principal Investigator

B. ____________________ Date: ___/___/___
Chairman, Institutional Human Subjects Research Review Committee